There are five titles in the 'Get Going With Creative Writing' series:

All About Me – 978-1-907733-90-1

Likes and Dislikes – 978-1-907733-91-8

Out and About – 978-1-907733-92-5

We Love Animals – 978-1-907733-93-2

What We Do – 978-1-907733-94-9

Guinea Pig Education
2 Cobs Way
New Haw, Addlestone
Surrey
KT15 3AF
Tel: 01932 336553
Website: www.guineapigeducation.co.uk

© Copyright 2014

NO part of this publication may be reproduced, stored or copied for commercial purposes and profit without the prior written permission of the publishers.

ISBN: 978-1-907733-91-8

Written: Sally A Jones and Amanda C Jones
Illustrations: Sally A Jones
Graphic Design: Annalisa Jones
USA Editing: S. Waller

Dear Kids,

Have fun learning to write with our 'Get Going With Creative Writing' series. Enjoy reading our short stories, some of which have been written by kids your age. Use our ideas to write your own stories, or try some non-fiction writing, such as, diaries, reports and leaflets. If you read or write well you will achieve high grades at school, so we challenge you to learn to love writing. You just need a notebook and pencil to start working through your guinea pig writing guide. Don't forget to color in the pictures.

....

Dear Teachers and Parents,

If your children think writing is dull, give them a guinea pig writing book from the 'Get Going With Creative Writing' series and we think they'll change their minds. However, these books are also ideal for those children who love to write, providing starting points that will make any budding young writer's imagination run wild, especially if they are preparing for standardized tests.

We have put together a series of themed books to inspire your child to write at his or her level. Whether you choose 'About Me,' 'We Love Animals,' 'Likes and Dislikes,' 'Out And About' or 'What We Do,' you will choose an English study book with a light-hearted, modern approach to appeal to the children of today.

The books can be used at home or in school alongside the existing curriculum. Inside, you will find a treasure trove of ideas for writing, featuring fiction and non-fiction themes. Based on the National Curriculum in the UK, they comply with respected strategies for literacy, with tips on planning and writing techniques, sentence construction, grammar tips and more.

Written by a former teacher, working as a tutor, the books have been tested by the children the author teaches in Surrey, England. These children agree the books are fun and help them learn to love writing.

We would like to thank the students of Guinea Pig Tuition – class of 2010/2011 – Sophia, Georgina, Harriet, Hannah, Sacha, Harry, Gareth, Rahan, Neena, Mahir, Neesha, Jai, Alexandra, Anna Maria and Vlad.

I absolutely hate horrible, big, hairy spiders that crawl and creep right up on you.

I'm lying on the floor reading a magazine, but I see something I don't like. It has a big, black body and eight long legs. It crawls across the carpet and up my pant leg at lightning speed. I move as if someone put a firework under me. I scream loudly. Dad comes running. When he finds me, I'm throwing everything off and standing there in my underwear.

Dad says calmly, "What's the matter?"
"There's a spider on my clothes. Catch it quickly before it gets away," I yell. Dad slowly moves off to get an empty jar to catch it in.

I see the spider again. Is it a tarantula? It has wide bulging eyes which stare up at me. It looks at me menacingly as if to say, 'You're scared of me aren't you? You know I can anesthetize a fly with my poisonous venom and eat it later for dinner.'
"Quick," I shout to my dad. "Come quickly!" The spider is startled and runs for cover under my chair so I scream loudly.

Then I leap off the chair. I sprint through the door, climb up the stairs and crouch in a safe hiding place on the landing. Dad is looking for the spider in the living room, but he can't find it. He moves the chair, but it's nowhere to be seen. One thing for sure, it will come back to haunt me later. I look down,
"AHHHHHH!"

How do you think the story will end? Write the ending.

Useful Writing Facts

- The story is written in present tense, as if it is happening now.

- The writer uses 'I,' so it is in first person.

- Dialogue moves the story along.

Now it is your turn to write.

- Do you like spiders?

- Write at least three sentences to explain why you like spiders or why you don't like spiders.

- Now ask your mom, dad, brother or sister, grandma or grandad or best friend if they like spiders. Write their answers.

Write a story about a time when a creepy crawly crept up on you.

Where were you? What happened? What did you do? Who helped you?

Write the story by choosing a suitable ending for each sentence.

Help write the slithery **snake** story.

Paragraph 1

At Reptile World, I am standing in front of a huge tank of sleepy reptiles. They are camouflaged in the…

- *long grass.*
- *dry sticks.*
- *yellow sand.*
- ....
- ....

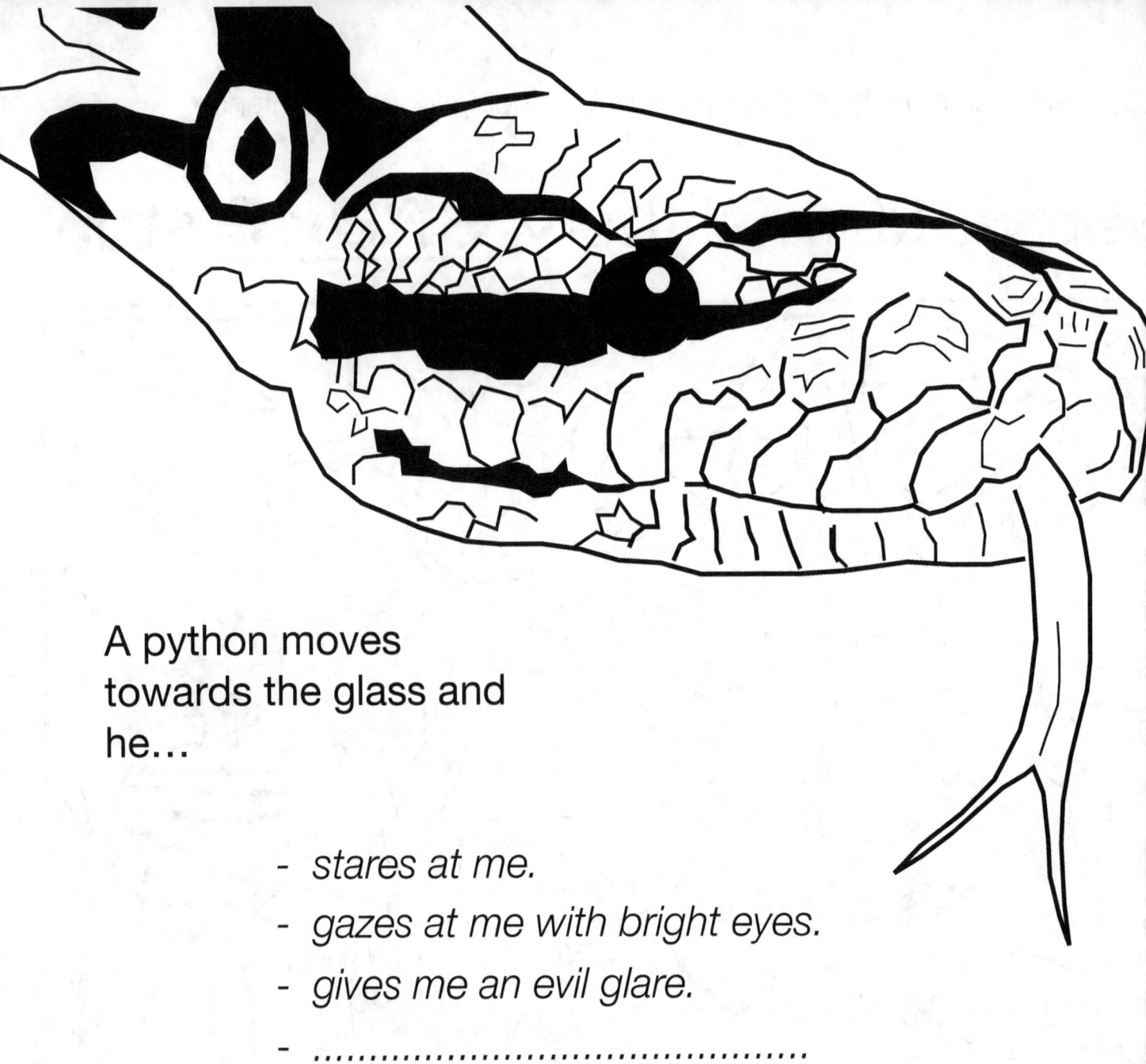

A python moves towards the glass and he…

- *stares at me.*
- *gazes at me with bright eyes.*
- *gives me an evil glare.*
- ………………………………………

Then he uncoils his powerful body showing…

- *his smooth snake skin.*
- *the patterns on his snake skin.*
- *how long he is.*
- ………………………………………………

He pokes out his forked tongue...

- *to hiss.*
- *to lick his lips.*
- *to show me he would like to swallow me whole.*
- ....

Paragraph 2

To my horror, I find myself being sucked into the cage and *taken/transported/...........* to a far away land.

It is the Amazon rainforest where…

- it is warm and humid.
- the rain pours down.
- I am running through a steamy jungle.
- ……………………………………………………………

I am…

- clambering through the shrub layers.
- shading under the canopy (of branches).
- searching the forest floor.
- ……………………………………………………………

There is a deafening noise…

- as parrots screech.
- as toucans squawk .
- as the rain pours down in torrents.
- as jaguars roar.
- as the anteaters snort and forage greedily for food.
- ……………………………………………………………

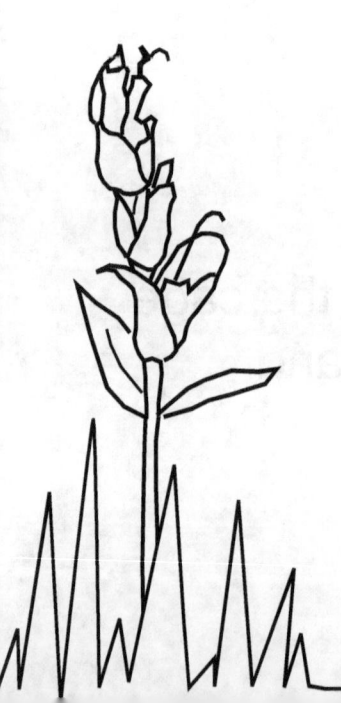

In the jungle, I see the same snake...

- *coming closer.*
- *opening his jaws wide*
- *about to strike me.*
- ....

Will he...

- *bite me.*
- *crush me.*
- *swallow me.*
- ....

I scream for Mom and Dad because I feel...

- *scared.*
- *terrified.*
- *petrified.*
- ....

At that moment...

- *an eagle swoops down.*
- *a playful monkey jumps out of the bushes.*
- *a fierce jaguar prowls past.*
- ....

The snake...

- *hesitates.*
- *stops moving.*
- *slithers back into the bushes.*
- ....

Paragraph 3

This gives me time to...

- *get away.*
- *scramble to safety.*
- *climb to a safe place.*
- ....

I close my eyes because...

- *I feel so tired,*
- *I feel very strange,*
- *I'm thinking of home,*
- ....

but, when I open them, I'm back at the tank where the snake…

- *is coiled up asleep.*
- *is in his hideout.*
- *is nowhere to be seen.*
- ………………………………………………………………

I say to Mom and Dad,

"I imagined what it was like…

- *to be inside the snake's cage."*
- *to be in the Amazon jungle."*
- *to be nearly bitten by a snake."*
- ………………………………………………………………

"Was it scary," they replied.

- *"No, not really," I whispered.*
- *"Not at all, nothing frightens me!" I boasted.*
- *"Just a bit," I giggled.*
- ………………………………………………………………

Do you <u>like</u> snakes?

- Write at least three sentences to explain why you like snakes or why you don't like snakes.

Now ask your mom, dad, brother, sister, grandma, grandad or best friend if they like snakes. Write their answers.

Your turn to write:

Imagine you are on vacation in Florida and you take a boat trip down the Everglades. You see crocs (crocodiles) and gators (alligators) swimming beside you. Write your own adventure story.

The Story Planner

The Story Planner will help you **_plan_ your story**. It will **_structure_ your story,** so it is organized into a beginning, middle and an ending.

Paragraph 1 is the introduction.

- The opening must make your reader want to read on.

- Introduce the characters and setting.
- Who are the people in the story? Where does it take place?

- Start the plot.

Paragraph 2 develops the story.

- Build up the plot with some action.

- Introduce problems to create tension.

- Build up suspense to make the reader wonder what will happen.

- Reach a crisis point.

Paragraph 3

- Wind the story up, showing how the problem is resolved.

- Choose a happy, sad or moral ending.

- Choose a cliffhanger ending - which leaves the reader to decide how it ends.

Who?
Your family takes a boat trip.

Where?
The Everglades in Florida

What happens?
A boy is messing around.

Develop the plot

* *boy hangs over the boat.*
* *falls over edge into water*
* *croc appears*
* *it is going to ...*
* *panic! everyone screams*

Wind the story up

* *boy is rescued*
* *everyone is relieved*
* *croc swims away*

Listen Live

Hi, I'm your D.J. George:

... and I'm Christabelle:

How are you today?

I'm good. How about you?

Well, I didn't sleep well last night.

Oh no! Why?

I had this terrible nightmare.

Tell me about it.

Well, I dreamed I was on vacation on The Gold Coast of Australia. It was amazing. The sun was beating down, so I went into the sea with the surfboard.

I was really enjoying riding the huge breakers (waves) on my board, when suddenly out of the corner of my eye, I spotted a black fin!

No! That must have been scary.

It got worse. I decided to get out as quickly as I could, but this creature moved purposefully towards me at an alarming speed. I saw its huge mouth open wide and then.... just as its teeth were about to sink into my flesh…. everything went dark and I woke up.

Oh no! That's awful.

It was so real that I was thankful to be back in my own bed.

Today I want you, the listeners, to send in your stories. Tell me about **what scares you**, what you have nightmares about or just tell me about the things you fear most. Contact us now.

In a restaurant, there was a big caterpillar crawling through my salad. It was disgusting! Even worse, the waiter removed the creature and then he expected me to continue eating my meal. I felt sick and I left the restaurant.

"How awful!"

I detest creatures that creep up on you. I screamed when I had an earwig in my bed and I went crazy when a wasp landed in my strawberry tart.

Priya writes…

I was flying to California to visit Disneyland and the plane flew through a huge thunder and lightning storm. It was bump, bump, bump for about an hour. The flight attendant was serving coffee and it spilled all over the floor. I was a bit alarmed.

Callum texts…

At night, the moon throws ghostly shadows across the lawn. I imagine the clothes-line looks like a scary monster standing there. I get scared so I hide under the covers.

"Oh no!"

"We have Max on the line.

Hello Max. What is your story?"

"Well, George, I was on a ferry in a gale and the waves were huge. The boat was tossing from side to side. It didn't do my stomach any good. Then a gigantic wave hit the boat and the lights went out. Worse than that, the china in the café crashed to the ground. It freaked me out, I can tell you."

"Wow! What a story."

| New | Reply | Reply all | Foward | Delete | Mark as ▼ | Move to ▼ |

INBOX (240)
FOLDERS
Junk (109)
Drafts (11)
Sent
Deleted (15)
New Folder

What Scares You

☐ **D.J. George** 1/15/15
   To George@guineapig.co.uk **Reply**

I am so scared of the dark that I imagine I hear footsteps on the landing and strange noises on the stairs. Then I imagine there's a ghost!

Charlotte

"I can't believe it."

Ryan emails...

I woke in the middle of the night to hear footsteps on the flat roof. I told my parents; they phoned the police. They caught a robber trying to break in.

"Oh no! That's horrific."

Dominic emails...

Sometimes I hear a train rattling along the railroad tracks. It sounds like an eerie ghost flying through the night.

Victoria has texted in...

I'm scared when the wind howls around the house, shaking the windows and doors.

Beatrice texts...

I am scared that a wild animal will come through my bedroom window so I keep it closed.

Ria writes...

A cat came through my bedroom window with a mouse in a trap in his mouth. Imagine waking up to that - it was horrible.

Jacob texts...

When there's a bad storm, I'm scared that the tree will crash down in my garden.

"There are some great stories here. Keep them coming in. Christabelle, let's hear about some of our listeners' most **terrifying dreams** now."

Isabel...

I dreamed that I got lost in the mountains. I was wandering around all night and could not find my way back.

"Spooky stuff"

Alex texts...

I dreamed that we had snails for school lunches and the lunchlady made us sit there until we had finished eating them.

Amy writes...

I dreamed an alien spacecraft landed and they took me into their craft. I was struggling to get away, because I was scared it would take off and fly me to some distant universe.

Daisy texts...

I dreamed that I lost my homework and my teacher made me clean the toilet as a punishment.

Jai has emailed...

I dreamed that I woke up as a girl and had to put on a dress. It was a shock.

Isaac has texted...

When I was asleep at my aunty's house, which is two hundred years old, I dreamed that I went back in time. In my bedroom, my laptop and T.V. had disappeared and there was only a pad of paper and an old fashioned pen on the desk. How would I cope? I looked out of the window in a panic, but everything had changed. My Dad's Jaguar was gone. There were no cars - only horses and carriages. The people were dressed in funny costumes. I was terrified. I was lost in time and would not be able to get back! What was I going to do? Then... I woke up!

> Why not try writing these stories. Use three paragraphs.

I am:

- frightened of going into our garden shed because big, black crawling things hide in there.

- scared a creepy crawly will crawl up my back and tickle me.

- afraid I might look down and see a big, black spider running up to me.

- scared I might put on my shoe and find something squelchy in there.

- frightened that a big, black fly will land on my food.

- terrified that a wasp will sting me.

- scared that I might swallow this big, hard candy whole.

- scared that I'll get locked in the bathroom or fall down a drain.

- fearful of: cats that hiss, rats with sharp teeth, bats that fly, dogs that jump and clowns that laugh and laugh.

- disgusted when I have to chew up sprouts.

- afraid that my friend's cat will jump on me or lick me.

- frightened of swarming ants because there are thousands of them and only one of me.

- scared that the school bully will tease me or steal my stuff.

- terrified of creaky noises after midnight, of ghosts, ghouls and horrible things that lurk in the dark.

- scared of sorting through boxes in the attic: you don't know what's in there.

Write an email, text or phone in to George. Write a paragraph to say what scares you or what you fear most. Now write some more sentences starting with 'I Am...".

I am loving:

- a relaxing bath full of soapy bubbles.

- stroking my soft cat's fur.

- sucking hard candies.

- munching marshmallows.

- ....

- ....

- ....

- ....

- ....

- ....

- ....

- ....

- ....

- ....

- ....

- ....

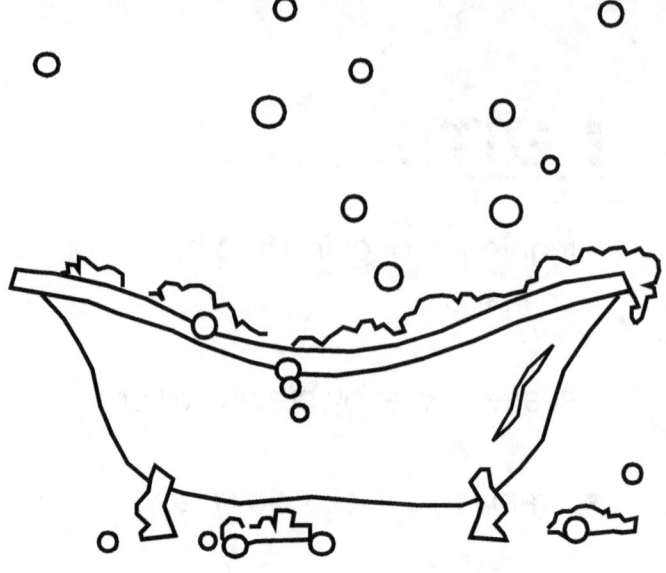

Now complete this page.

Write a story. Call it...

'Swim for your life.'

Use the story planner to plan your story.

Ask:

- **Where was I?**
- **Why was I there?**
- **How did I get there?**
- **What was the weather like?**
- **Who was I with?**

Remember: The introduction sets the scene, introduces characters and begins the plot.

- **What happens next?**
- **..and then...?**
- **...and after that...?**

Describe the events in order.

Introduce a problem to create tension and suspense as you continue the plot. Use short sentences to create a feeling of shock.

Look out! Turn around! Panic!

- **How does the story end?**

Wind the story up... with a happy, sad or moral ending or a cliffhanger ending.

For example:

Happy Ending

1. Swim fast to escape

2. Grab a rope and get hauled into a boat

3. Feel relief that you have reached the beach.

Moral Ending

Don't stray too far from the shore when you are surfing or swimming or don't go far out to sea on a float.

Swim for your Life

I hadn't a care in the world that day, but this was going to change. It was a boiling hot, sunny day so I decided to take my surfboard into the ocean. I quickly changed into my wetsuit, waded into the crystal clear water and splashed around amongst the colorful tropical fish. I felt the straggly underwater weed, that clings to the seabed, brush against my feet.

To start with, I stayed near the beach and enjoyed riding the breakers as they crashed onto the shore. After a while, I decided to go further out into the deeper water to ride the bigger waves. It felt good out there. The waves were huge. I prepared to ride a big wave on my surfboard, but... suddenly... I became aware that there was something else in the water close to me. I was sure it was not another surfer. It was casting a dark shadow over me. As I turned, I saw it there. It was the black fin of a shark. I screamed... help! help! help!

The next five minutes are a blur in my mind. I remember seeing the open jaw, the row of sharp teeth and the ferocious look in the creature's eye. I remember hearing people shout from the beach, "Shark attack! Alert the lifeguard." Then I remember swimming faster than ever before towards the beach. I remember someone grabbing hold of my hand, dragging me out of the water and laying me down on a blanket. To my relief I heard the rescue team say,
"He's unhurt, it didn't get him, but he's lucky to be alive."

Write the story of George's dream.

Write a moral ending for the last sentence.

"Ghosts Are Scary," Says Sam.

They are:

scary	frightening	terrifying	petrifying	fearsome
dark	black	hideous	spooky	creepy
eerie	haunting	jittery	uncanny	unearthly
weird	strange	monstrous	grim	ghostly
hair raising	alarming	blood curdling	grisly	gruesome
horrible	horrifying	shocking	terrible	startling
menacing	formidable	sinister	unnatural	corpse like
deathly	supernatural	spectral	shadowy	

If I think I see one, I am:

panic-stricken   dumbstruck   frozen to the spot

Can you think of any more ghostly words? *Use a thesaurus to help you.*

Copy the chart into your notebook. Can you make up any more?

Describing Words **Adjectives**	Naming Words **Nouns**	Action Words **Verbs**	Describing the action words **Adverbs**
scary	ghost	haunts	spookily
hungry	shark	moves	purposefully
black	spider	scuttles	quickly
slimy	snake	slithers	slowly
huge	wave	crashes	violently
big	caterpillar	munches	greedily
hot	chocolate	spills	messily

Are *you* <u>**afraid**</u> of the **DARK**?

- Write down some things that make you afraid of the dark.

- Now write at least three sentences to explain why you are afraid.

I'm afraid of:

creaky doors that ....

noises the central heating pipes make ....

all strange noises because I think..

trains rushing past ....

owls hooting in the tree ....

foxes barking ....

I love soccer

Frank would like to be a professional soccer player and play for his country. He reads an article about a famous player, 'Bobby,' in the newspaper.
How did Bobby learn to play so well?

> "Bobby first played soccer on his school team. Then he played for his youth team in the evening, but he was so good that he was chosen to play for a professional team," reads Frank aloud.

"Wow," said Sam, "what did he do next?"

> "After this, he scored twenty goals in ten games."

"That's amazing," adds Sam.

> "Later, he became a manager for a professional team and he helped them climb to the top of their league. He brought in lots of famous players."

"and after that..."

> "In the end he became a manager for a team in England. His team nearly won the semi-final match in the World Cup."

"Never!"

> "They only lost the game on penalties. Then they would have played the winning team. His team might have won the World Cup."

Answer the questions in sentences.

1. By whom was Bobby chosen to play football?

   ....

2. How many goals did he score in 10 games?

   ....

3. What job was he chosen for?

   ....

4. Which country was he manager for?

   ....

5. Why did England lose the World Cup?

   ....

Sam listens to the sports commentary on *Guinea Pig FM* radio. He listens to a **soccer commentary**.

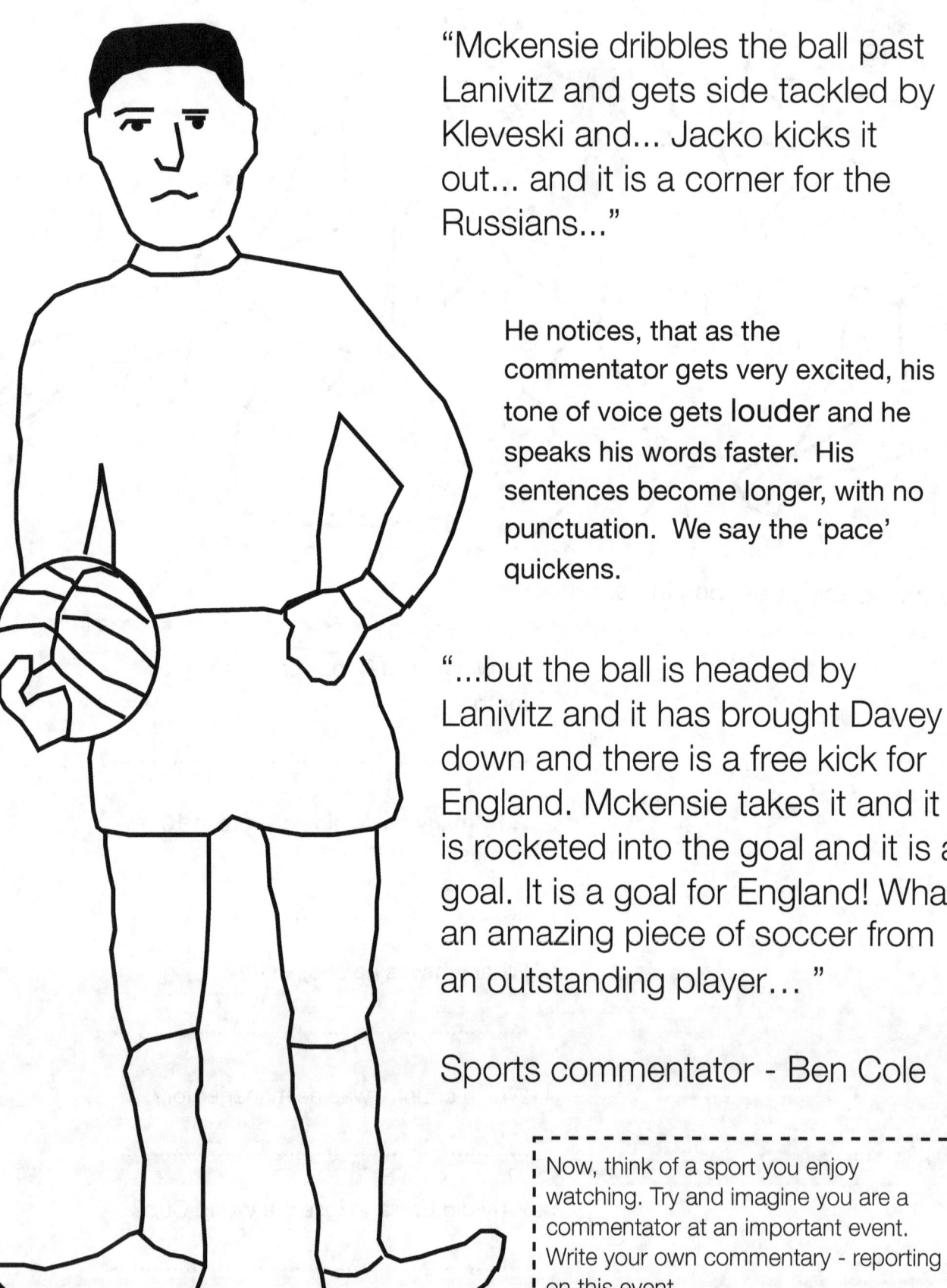

"Mckensie dribbles the ball past Lanivitz and gets side tackled by Kleveski and... Jacko kicks it out... and it is a corner for the Russians..."

He notices, that as the commentator gets very excited, his tone of voice gets louder and he speaks his words faster. His sentences become longer, with no punctuation. We say the 'pace' quickens.

"...but the ball is headed by Lanivitz and it has brought Davey down and there is a free kick for England. Mckensie takes it and it is rocketed into the goal and it is a goal. It is a goal for England! What an amazing piece of soccer from an outstanding player… "

Sports commentator - Ben Cole

> Now, think of a sport you enjoy watching. Try and imagine you are a commentator at an important event. Write your own commentary - reporting on this event.

Think about a game you would like to play...

What is the game?

Write down some instructions on how to play it.

What equipment do you need to play?

Who do you play with?

How many people can play?

How long does the game take to play?

Do you compete against other teams or individuals?

What do you win?

Would you like to compete in a world competition, like the Olympic Games?

What famous sportsmen or women do you know?

They can be football players, racecar drivers and golf stars for example.

Look up your athlete on the internet or in a reference book. Find the answers to the questions below.

- What age did (.....) start playing?

- Did (.....) compete for a school or youth team?

- What team does (.....) play for now?

- How long has your sports person been competing/playing?

- What age is (.....)?

- How did (.....) achieve success?

- How many awards or medals has (.....) won?

- Write ten facts about your chosen sports celebrity.

Now imagine a day in the life of your athlete.
What would it be like? Write:
'A day in the life of ...'

SPORTY Magazine Mailbag

Invites its readers to write about the sports they play.

Star Letter

When I first had Zack my horse, he was very difficult to handle, because he would rear up, spin around and refuse to come out of his stable. We have had to work hard with my trainer.

It has paid off. This month he has done wonderfully in the Junior Riding Championships which are held over a few days. He jumped all the fences and didn't knock any of the poles down. I rode well in my first round so we were able to compete in the jump off against the clock. My horse jumped another clear round and he had the fastest time. We came in first; I was so excited.

Zack was presented with a lovely blue rosette by the president of The Horse Society. What a very special horse he is. He is fearless on the show jumping course, but at home, when he's with me, he's so good natured and such great fun.

Jess, by email

I am on the diving team at my gym. Every morning, I get up at six to practice my diving at the pool. I don't have much spare time for other interests, as my coach enters me for competitions which are held on weekends. There's a lot of waiting around between dives, but then my turn comes and I go up to take my position. Next, I stretch up my arms and think about my dive because I have to get it right. Before a competition you have to get plenty of sleep, so you are focused and dive safely.

Louis

Write in. We want to hear about you, about the sports you play and how you keep fit.

Jess **BRAINSTORMS**

Imagine Jessica's horse

Draw him in his stable.	**Draw Jess.**

Zack is: **but he is also:**

bold	confident	hard to handle	naughty
cocky	independent	mischievous	timid
inquisitive	fearless	stubborn	angry
fun	good natured	grumpy	fierce

Jess belongs to the pony club. To ride her horse, she needs to put a saddle and a bridle on him. Jess wears a special riding helmet. She trains or schools him to compete in competitions. He competes in dressage events, cross jumping events and show jumping events. When she rides him, he can gallop, trot or canter. In the show jumping ring there will be high fences, laid out in a course. It might include a high wall or a water jump. If Zack knocks down a fence in the competition, the poles will come down and he will get four faults for each one he knocks down. If he refuses to jump, he will get three faults. If he jumps all the fences, he will get a clear round. If he jumps the next round against the clock and gets the fastest time and the fewest faults, he will be the winner. Then he will be presented with a rosette or a medal.

Jess, and her horse Zack, jump the fences at a show jumping competition.

Put her thoughts in order as she competes. Choose which thoughts you want to use. For example:

(1) We've got ten minutes to warm up before we go into the ring.
(2) ....
(3) ....
(4) ....
(5) ....
Can you continue…

Oh no! He refused to jump - that's three faults.

My horse gets excited at championships so he can't concentrate.

I get so scared; it ruins my performance.

Yippee! We're in the next round!

We've only got ten minutes to warm up before we go in the ring.

I find it hard to remember the show jumping course.

My horse is slow against the clock in the jump off.

I'm so excited because I got a clear round.

I can't believe we've won a rosette.

Here we go, it's time to go into the ring.

Oh no! Did we knock that fence down and get four faults? Has the pole come down?

Come on Zack. You've got to put in your best effort in this competition.

Help! This fence is very high.

Let's collect some sporty words or phrases. Can you add words to these lists...

S
P
O
R
T
Y

When Sam plays soccer, he can: *kick, pass, head, run after, score a goal, take a penalty with the ball.* **The Players:** *run up and down the field, pass the ball and tackle each other.* **The goal keeper:** *misses/catches the ball, stops the goal.* **The spectators:** *cheer and chant in the stadium.*

When Beth practices her swimming, *she swims up and down the lanes, doing: breast stroke, front crawl, butterfly and back stroke, to get the fastest time.*

When Sonny plays tennis: *he hits the ball back and forward across the court with his racket. His opponent hits the ball back with force. They score 15 love, 30 love. It's a tie. The winning player must score 2 more points to get deuce. The umpire shouts game, set and match. The winner collects his trophy. The ball boys and girls collect up the tennis balls.*

When Naveed practices his gymnastics, he does: *handstands, cartwheels, back flips and somersaults on the mat. He balances on the highest beam.*

You have found out that **each sport** has its own **technical words**. What words do other sports use? (ballet, basketball, volleyball, cricket, karate, boxing or rugby for example.) Make some more lists.

Write an interesting article about the sport you play for Sporty Magazine. Include lots of detail to make the writing interesting for the reader.

Why is it important to take part in sports?

Complete: It is important to have plenty of exercise because...........

Sporty Magazine

wants to know what sports you do in school and out of school.

Write about the sport you play:

Present tense

- I *(take part in)* ....

    (compete in) ....

    (do) ....

    (enjoy) ....

- I choose this sport because ....

- Every *day/ week/ month* I have to ....

- This is what I do when I take part in my *class/sport* ....

- First I ....

- After that ....

- Next ....

- Then ....

- Finally ....

- At the end of the session I ....

- Sometimes I take part in *a competition* ....

    an event .... at ....

    a show ....

Past tense

- This is what I did ....

    ....

Melissa Montague's Dancing Lessons

Ballet, tap, modern, jazz, and disco dance.

Where: Mowtown Methodist Church Hall

When: Wednesday from 5 - 7pm.

> Melissa Montague, a former ballerina with the Royal Ballet Company, invites you to attend her amazing dance classes and achieve excellence in dance.
>
> She offers:
>
> - Top grades in all your exams.
> - A leading part in her show.
> - No favoritism.
> - Your own agent to help you on your way to stardom.
> - A possible career on the stage.
> - Parts in plays and other top Broadway shows.

Now make a poster for your own school.

.... School of ....
In: ....
At: ....
On: ....

He/She offers: ....
....
....

We love to dance...
well, most of the time!

The kids at Melissa Montague's dancing academy have practiced for weeks for the exam. Now the day has come and they must show the tester that they know their dance routines. We join them in the dressing room.

"Watch out, don't spill that gel, Amber," I yell as I pull on my pale blue leotard, but it is too late. A great dollop of sticky gel lands with a plop on the front of my costume.
"I'm really sorry, Yasmin."
"Quick, wipe it off, before it stains," says Amber's mom, leaping to the rescue with a wad of tissues.
"Ahh, Mom, don't pull my hair so tight. It hurts."
"Stop fussing, Yasmin," replies Mom as she twists my ponytail up into a neat bun on top of my head and stabs pins into it.
"You're stabbing me with those pins."
"Don't be silly…"
"Sh, sh, sh – keep the noise down," whispers the dancing teacher.

A few minutes later, Amber, Jamie and I are standing by the door of the hall waiting to go in and meet the tester.
"I feel sick," whispers Jamie to Amber.
"Me too."
The other kids shuffle around, tapping their toes loudly on the wooden floor. The door opens and Jamie makes a face.
"Can't remember a thing!"
"It's just nerves. You'll be fine."

We take up our positions while the tester sits at a long desk writing. Amber and I exchange glances. We want to giggle, but we have to stop ourselves. The lady tester is wearing a hat with a feather. We run through our routines. All is going well. Then suddenly… Amber slips, she loses her balance and falls on the floor. It's all going wrong. Thoughts buzz through her head as she fights back the tears. I won't pass. I've messed it all up – she thinks.

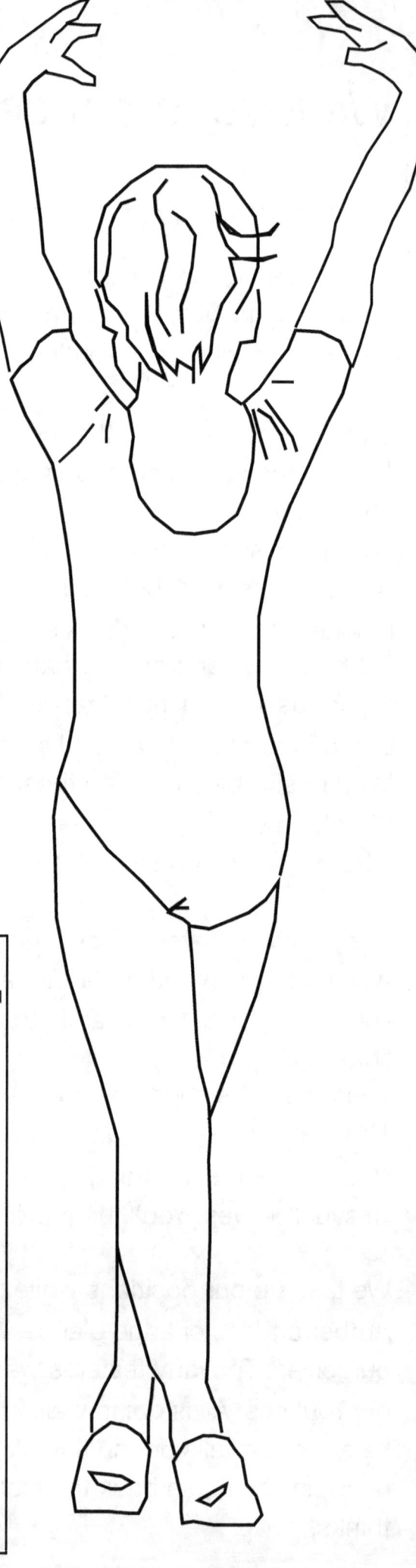

The lady tester pauses from her writing and looks up.
"Don't worry dear, I'll put the C.D. on again." She says with a reassuring smile, "Try again dear," and she spends several seconds writing.

Soon the exam is over and we spill out of the room, chatting excitedly.
"That was awful! What will Miss Montague say? Do you think I'll fail?"
"If you think that was bad – I got all my steps wrong. Didn't you see me?"
"How did it go darling?" asks Mom.
"Fine," I say. "Just fine." We change back into our jeans and sweatshirts and pack up our dancing gear and head off to the café over the road for a smoothie.

> If you write in first person (I) – you get the main character's view of what's happening in the story. If you write in third person (he/she), it is like being a fly on the wall and you get the watcher's view. Dialogue is used to move the story along. Use a new line for each new speaker.
>
> Have you ever done an exam - in dance, music, piano, or swimming? Write the story.
>
> - What type of exam did you do?
> - What was the tester like?
> - How did you feel as you went in?
> - What did he or she say?
> - How did the exam go?
> - Did you make mistakes or fall over?
> - Did you think you had passed?
> - What result did you get?

Read the story, We Love To Dance.

Did you notice that the story is moved on by the characters speaking to each other? It is moved on by dialogue.

Your turn to write:

Write a story about taking a test. It could be to test your skill – in music, piano, dance or karate or just a test in literacy, math or science.

(1) I have (had) been practicing for weeks for my test in ...

(2) A few minutes later, I am (was) standing by the door waiting to go in ...

(3) Soon the test is (was) over and we rush (rushed) out of ...

Write 3-5 sentences for each paragraph.

Use **dialogue** to move the story on.

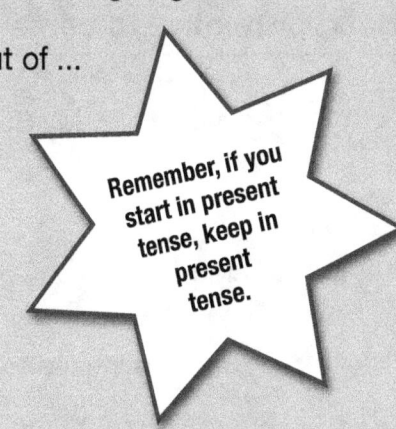

Remember, if you start in present tense, keep in present tense.

Use **first person.**

BEFORE: Describe characters, setting, and getting ready for the test.

DURING: Describe during the test, the actions and problems.

AFTER: Describe how you felt afterwards.

Now let's think about Sports Day at school.

Write a list of all the races you could compete in:

running	relay	hurdle
bean bag	wheel-barrow	three legged
obstacle	sack	sprinting

Tick three races that you have competed in or would like to compete in.

Write a letter inviting your parents, a friend or relative to come and watch.

My School Address,
The date

Dear Mr. and Mrs. ...,

You are invited to our .... at .... on ....

....

The races will start at .... Your son/daughter will be in ....

....
....
....

At the end of the afternoon refreshments will be served at ....

....

.... We hope you will be able to attend.

Yours sincerely,
Teacher

Write the story of your sports day.

At one thirty I...
....
....

Now, I was going to compete in the............
....
....

By the end of the afternoon, I felt...............
....
....

Remember:

- Write 3-5 sentences
- Write in first person
- Write about your chosen races in 3 paragraphs.

Sports day

I loved everything about sports day at Rushford Junior High School. It was the best day of the spring semester. At exactly three thirty sharp on sports day, the classes carried chairs out to the field and took up their positions. The teachers started to call out names and we lined up in groups for our races. Before I knew it, I was standing on the starting line waiting to compete in my first race, the obstacle race. Then, I was racing up to the line; grabbing a beanbag, running back to put it in the bucket, zooming back to get another, going back to the bucket and on to the finishing line. After this, I felt something smack me 'bang' in the eye. I slowed down: Lucy, the new girl, zoomed past me and beat me to the finish line.

Now it was time for Ethan and I to do the three-legged race. That means we had two of our legs tied together with a scarf, so we only had three legs between us and we were lolloping along the track together in the lead. We were going to win, when Ethan stumbled and we both toppled towards the ground falling in a heap on the floor. We came last, of course. I had one more chance to come first in the running race. I raced with all my strength, getting faster... and faster... and even faster.... The finish line was in view, but then something strange happened. An arm from another competitor knocked into me. It made me stumble. I nearly fell. As I tried to regain my speed, Lucy raced past me again and came first.

By the end of the afternoon, dark clouds had moved in as if there was going to be a storm. Even the parents' race didn't seem funny any more. I went up to the podium to receive a green ribbon for third prize in the obstacle race; I still felt bad – really bad. Now it was time to present the ribbon for running. "It's unfair," I spoke aloud: "Lucy cheated." To my surprise, a PTA member stood up and made an announcement to the school.
"We can't present a prize for the running because the winner has been disqualified," she exclaimed. "We will run the race again." This is exactly what happened but guess who won? Yes, it was me, Chloe, of course!

Think

Does your school do a sports day?
Do you compete in races?
What happened in your 1st, 2nd, 3rd races?
Who presented the prize?
What did your Mom or Dad say?

When? Where? Who came?
Which ones?
Did you win or come last?
How did you feel?

> Mrs. Barker says to her class, "Choose a sport you take part in: basketball, football, hockey, cricket, swimming, gymnastics."

1. Imagine you are in a lesson. Write down some instructions that your teacher gives you in the lesson.

    - I want you to hold on to the bar and kick your feet.
    - ....
    - ....

2. Write about what you wear.

3. Write about the equipment you need.

4. Write about the best thing you have done in your sport.

    - I love ....

5. Write about the worst thing that happened in your sport.

    - I hate ....

You have been chosen to represent your school. How do you feel? Write what happened.

Write a letter to your parents inviting them to watch you compete.

Things I love about the pool...

... and things I hate

Splashing around in the pool is always fun.

Jumping in the cool water is quite refreshing.

Moving fast up the pool, practicing the front crawl, is awesome.

Competing in races is cool, especially if you win.

Gliding and diving like a fish and getting a brick from the bottom of the pool is great.

Practicing life saving skills, in my pajamas, is an important skill to learn.

I hate chlorine in my eyes because it always stings like mad...

and if I get water in my ears it makes them pop.

Wet hair, on a cold day, makes me shiver...

and it's always warmer getting changed into my bathing suit than getting dressed.

We love plays

In our town, it is popular for the whole family to go to the theater to see a play during holidays and summer vacation. The theater shows many different kinds of plays. The stories are often taken from folk tales or fairy tales. Popular plays are Puss in Boots, Aladdin, and Jack and the Beanstalk.

Sometimes these plays star famous celebrities who come to town to perform just for us. Other times, there are local actors and actresses starring in the shows. Everyone wears colorful costumes. There are beautiful sets painted like distant and magical lands

These plays are often light-hearted comedies and contain humor that appeals to adults and children. Sometimes, there is even a character on stage encouraging the audience to participate: to shout, clap or boo. The audience will call out 'It's over there' or 'It's behind you' or they'll repeat 'Oh yes we do' or 'Oh no we didn't!' The audience is encouraged to 'boo' the villains and 'aww' the poor victim. Our town plays are lively shows.

Here are some well-known folk stories and fairytales. Can you match the settings, plots and characters?

Cinderella
Snow White
Aladdin
Jack and the Beanstalk

In this story:

★ The hero's mother has to sell Daisy, the cow, because they are so poor.
★ The hero swaps Daisy for a bag of beans.
★ His mom is angry and throws them into the garden.
★ The beans grow up and up, as high as a giant's castle.
★ The hero climbs up the beanstalk and he defeats the giant to win a pot of gold.
★ The hero lives happily ever after.

In this story:

★ The heroine's evil stepmother wants her dead because she is so beautiful.
★ The girl is taken to the woods.
★ She escapes and lives with seven dwarves.
★ The stepmother believes her stepdaughter is dead.
★ She asks the magic mirror, 'Who is the most beautiful of them all?'
★ The mirror tells the truth so the stepmother knows the girl is not dead.
★ The stepmother is very angry so disguises herself as an old woman selling apples.
★ She sells her stepdaughter a poisoned apple.
★ The girl eats the apple and collapses.
★ She is brought back to life by a kiss from a handsome prince.
★ They marry and live happily ever after.

In this story:

★ A girl works as a servant for her evil stepmother and ugly sisters.
★ They are all invited to a ball.
★ The girl is not able to go because she has to cook, clean and has nothing to wear.
★ A fairy godmother appears and waves her magic wand to make a beautiful gown and a horse and carriage.
★ The heroine goes to the ball.
★ A prince falls in love with her.
★ At midnight she has to leave.
★ The magic gown turns to rags.
★ She leaves behind a glass slipper.
★ The prince searches the land for the girl who fits the shoe.
★ The prince is reunited with the heroine and they marry.

In this story:

★ A poor laundry boy falls in love with the Emperor's daughter.
★ To win her hand, he has to become rich.
★ He must battle against Abanazar, the evil Sorcerer, but is helped by a genie in a lamp.
★ He goes into a magic cave of jewels.
★ He becomes rich and marries the Emperor's daughter.

Write about your visit to a play or write about your favorite play

Which play did you see?

....
....

Where did you go?

....
....

Who was in it?

....
....

Who are the characters?

....
....

Where does it take place?

....
....

What is the plot?

....
....

How does it end?

....
....

What was your favorite part?

....
....

Now read the script called:

The Skull and Crossbone

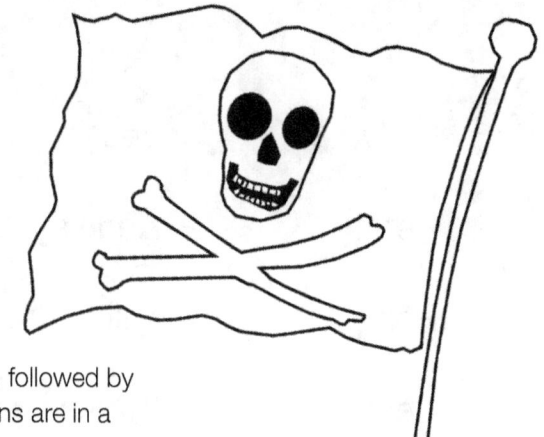

A play script is in present tense. The characters' names are on the left, followed by a colon:. What they say has no quotation marks and the stage directions are in a different font. Actions are in brackets. New characters have a new line.

Scene 1: Starts on the sea somewhere north of Australia.

Pete: Let's introduce ourselves to the boys and girls, Polly.

Polly: Hello, Hello. I'm pretty Polly and I'm a pirate's parrot, so I sit on his shoulder.

He's Pirate Pete, a pirate on our ship, the Skull and Crossbone.

Pete: They'll know I'm a pirate, Polly, because I have a bandana around my head and baggy shorts and…

Polly: No, they won't because you don't have a patch over your eye.

Pete: Not all pirates wear patches.

Polly: No, but they have a hook for a hand, a peg leg and a sword … and you don't have any of these…

Pete: I'm a nice pirate, you know that Polly. I'm only here because the Skull and Crossbone plundered my ship and took me prisoner. I'll never see my friends again or my true love.

(wipes a tear from his eye)

Polly: You have to be mean to be a pirate…

Pete: …and have a deep throaty voice.

Polly: Yes

Pete: And say 'Come on me hearties' and all that pirate stuff...

Polly: ...like a real pirate

Pete: We know that I'm planning to escape when we get to port and you'll be coming with me.

Polly: But... but I like it at sea.

Pete: No, Polly, you'll like it on land.

Polly: Oh no, I won't

Pete: Oh yes, she will. Won't she boys and girls?

Polly: No I won't

(audience join in)

Pete: Oh yes, you will

(The noise of heavy footsteps can be heard coming up onto the deck. The pirate quickly starts to get on with his work. Enter Captain Bloodthirsty – a fearsome looking man with a thick beard and black eyes.)

Pete: It's the captain and he's in one of his moods.

Captain Bloodthirsty: What's going on up here? You've been standing idle. Where's the rest of the crew? First mate, get them working.

First mate: Ay, Ay Sir

Dangerous Dan, my lad, scrub the deck until it shines. Terrifying Toby, get up to the top of that mast and start looking out.

Terrifying Toby:	Ay, Ay Sir
Captain Bloodthirsty:	No one messes with me, Captain Bloodthirsty. I've got a sword in my hand, a pistol in my belt and I'm ready to fight. Did you know that?
All Pirates:	Ay, Ay Captain. We're all ready to fight.

Scene 2: The pirates sit around eating and drinking mugs of rum, except for Terrifying Toby who is keeping look out at the top of the mast.

Captain Bloodthirsty:	Eat up, my lad. Don't sneer at good food.
Pete:	It's too salty, Sir. I can't eat it.
Captain Bloodthirsty:	How dare you insult the food on the Skull and Crossbone. We've traveled 900 miles with this cook. Cook! Pirate Pete says this meat is too salty.
Cook:	It's all we've got, Sir. It's what we stole from the H.M.S. Victory. Get eating it. Don't mess around with the captain. You don't know how lucky you are. We've got supplies plundered from all the navy's best boats. We've got all their treasure.
Dangerous Dan:	We got oat biscuits full of maggots.

Cook: Them maggots are good for you. They provide you with protein me boys.

Dangerous Dan: They taste YUK!

When you bite into them, you can feel the blighters crunch beneath your teeth.

Captain Bloodthirsty: Eat up. No one grumbles on the Skull and Crossbone and lives to tell the tale.

Pirate 1: We sing and dance our sea shanties into the night to the sound of the pipe.

(The men break into a jolly song …Yo Ho Ho and a bottle of rum.)

Pirate 2: …and then we go to bed and dream of plundering ships and all the goodies and treasures we'll get.

Captain Bloodthirsty: …and the fine gentlemen's clothes I'll steal, from real gentlemen, so that when we anchor up and go ashore, I go into town looking like a rich man.

(Suddenly, there is a cry from above and the sound of scrambling down the stairs. Terrifying Toby's face appears around the door.)

Terrifying Toby: Sir, Sir, there's a ship on the horizon. It looks like a big one. A real prize Sir.

Captain Bloodthirsty: All men at the ready. Haul up the sails, me hearties, to increase our speed. We'll track her and…then…at midnight we'll attack – when she least expects it.

Pete: Oh no, Polly, I can't bear this. They'll creep up on another fine ship. They'll rob it and then sink it to the depths of the ocean. The crew will be in danger.

(Captain Bloodthirsty is up on the bridge looking through his telescope.)

Captain Bloodthirsty: Shiver me timbers. There she is... a fine ship on the horizon. She'll be carrying a fortune of treasure.

Raise the flag me lads. Get the Jolly Roger up. We'll show them we mean business.

1st pirate mate: Full speed ahead. Get ready for attack. Fire up the cannons. Fire after three… 1, 2, 3….

Tom the Terrible: They're firing back. Let off another cannon. We'll show them. No ship gets the better of the Skull and Crossbone.

(There is a strong smell of burning timber.)

Pete: Oh no, Polly, I can't see through the thick black smoke and I'm frightened. I'm just not cut out for being a pirate.

Polly: Keep me on your shoulder.

Captain Bloodthirsty: Lower the rowing boats. We're going aboard.

(The pirates board their prize together.)

Scene 3

Captain Bloodthirsty:
(in an aggressive tone)

Surrender or you'll regret it!

Your ship is now under pirate control.

Line up your men. If you don't join us pirates, you will walk the plank and we'll leave you in the shark infested sea to swim home.

(The crew of H.M.S. England surrender and obey instructions.)
(Turning to crew with a beaming smile.)

Me jolly hearties and fellow pirates, get ready to search the boat for loot. Take everything. Leave no treasure behind. Take it all and bring it back to the Skull and Crossbone.

(Back on the Skull and Crossbone.)

First Pirate Mate:

Steer the ship towards Treasure Island. We've got our work cut out burying all this treasure.

Well done me hearties. We're going to be rich men, when we come back for it.

Continue the play script. Write how the pirate crew of the Skull and Crossbone go to Treasure Island, how Pete escapes with Polly, how the pirates get their just desserts, how Pete gets all the money and how he gets home and marries his true love. Play continues in a few pages.

★ <u>**Plan**</u> and <u>**write**</u> your own **pirate play**.

★ Think about **characters, setting** and **plot**.

★ Think about **action, suspense** and **tension**.

★ Think about how to **keep the audience interested**.

We love to imagine...

Close your eyes. Picture a pirate...

- What does your pirate look like?

- How is he dressed?

- What does his pirate vessel look like?

- What does he say?

- What is his character like?

- What does he do?

This pirate vocabulary will help you:

raise a flag	chase a ship	fire the guns
board the ship	search for treasure	take prisoners
hoist The Jolly Roger	commence a fierce battle	

Paragraph 1

Imagine a pirate ship sailing on the high sea. What does it look like? The pirate flag, The Jolly Roger, is hoisted. There's a prize up ahead (a sailing ship).

Paragraph 2

A sea battle takes place between pirates and sailors. Cannons are fired. The pirates board the ship and take prisoners from the crew. They steal loot from the ship. What do they do next?

Paragraph 3

Write about the treasure. Does it contain gold, silver, precious jewels and fine clothes? What do the pirates do with the treasure? Where do they hide it? Do they hide it on an island? Do they share it?

Write an adventure story.

We love tropical beaches with white sand and palm trees, but we are scared of pirates.

Imagine that you have been shipwrecked on a desert island. Write the story of your adventure. Who did you meet? What happened? How did you manage to survive? What events led to your rescue?

uninhabited	deserted	shipwreck
tropical	mountains	palm trees
coconuts	parrots	jungle
fishing	hunting	raft
light fire	pirates	buried treasure
clues	tracks	caves
map	rescue	ship

Use the vocabulary above and the tips on the next page to help you.

Beginning: Set the scene

Imagine that you are stranded on a desert island.

- How did you become stranded on a desert island?
- What island were you on?
- How did you survive?
- What did you eat?
- Where did you sleep?

Middle: Build up events to a climax

- Write about an adventure you had.
- Who did you meet? What happened?
- You found an old map.
- You dug up treasure and found a chest full of gold and precious jewels.

Ending: Wind the story up to a good conclusion.

- How were you rescued?
- What did you do with the treasure when you got home?

Use the words and phrases on the next page to make your story interesting.

Now draw a map of the island. Mark on the map where the shipwreck/plane crash occurred. Write about: where you slept, where you lived and any other places of special interest on the island.

boat	shipwreck	plane crash

Characters:

me	animals	pirates
parrots	exotic animals like kiwis	

Setting:

hot	tropical island	

Which actions:

catch eels in the river	cook on the fire I have made	collect wood to make a fire
wash in a stream	sleep in a hammock made of leaves	build a shelter
catch insects or small animals to eat	use salvage from the shipwreck	keep unusual island pets
boil water on a fire to make it clean to drink	swim amongst eels	live amongst snakes
fight off flies	get used to big spiders in your bed	see a rescue boat
see a helicopter searching	me - reported missing	search the horizon for help - waves arms

Which words:

uninhabited	deserted	shipwreck
pirates	buried treasure	map
tracks	clues	coconuts
palm trees	tropical	jungle
mountains	eat coconuts	look out for natives
explore the island	look out for danger	

Plan

Remember Pirate Pete and his crew. How does the play end?

Scene 4

- The pirates anchor their boat near Treasure Island.
- They choose a place to bury the treasure.
- They start to dig.
  Horrible creatures take turns making life difficult: crocodile, spider, monkey.
- Black Jim, an old pirate, appears. He has been living on the island.
- He claims all the treasure belongs to him.

Scene 5

- A fight breaks out between the two old enemies – Black Jim and Captain Bloodthirsty and his crew.
- Meanwhile, a giant crab lets the prisoners free.
- A lobster chases some of the pirates round the stage.
- A monkey steals the key to the treasure chest. He spills money from the chest and sits on it.
- The prisoners join on Black Jim's side and fight Captain Bloodthirsty.

Scene 6

- Pete and Polly see their chance to escape.
- They lower the skull and crossbones and hoist the ship's sails, while the pirates are fighting.
- Polly goes back and collects as much of the treasure as she can.
- Now, Polly squawks to all the prisoners to come back on board because the boat is ready to sail.
- They sail the high sea and Black Jim and Captain Bloodthirsty are left marooned on the island.
- They sail to England where Pete marries his sweetheart.
- The play ends with the couple reunited and a wedding.

...and now the conclusion to The Skull And Crossbone. Fill in the speakers' missing words.

(The pirates drop anchor off Treasure Island. They stand in a ring on the sand discussing where they will bury the treasure. The prisoners are tied up with rope. Pete and Polly whisper together behind a bush.)

Pete: *(from behind a palm tree)* A treasure island. How exciting! It smells like one.

Polly: *(flies off to grab some leaves in her beak.)* It even tastes like one.

Captain B: Drop the anchor.

Dangerous Dan: Ay, Ay Captain...

Captain B: Well done, me maties! We'll bury the treasure and then we'll break open the rum and party.

Dangerous Dan: I'll mark the hiding place on me map with a cross. One day we'll come back and be rich men. Just think of all those fine things rich gentlemen have.

Captain B: We'll see about that. I've got the treasure now. IT'S ALL MINE. No one can get it from me. Captain Bloodthirsty will be rich. He'll be a fine gentleman. *(raises voice)*

Pirates: What about the rest of us? It's not fair. He's cheating us. Let's start a mutiny.

Captain B: I'll give you one coin each if you work hard. Take the bootie and dig a hole me maties - NOW or else....

We must get my treasure buried before it gets dark. (agitated)

(Suddenly a terrifying pirate appears menacingly with ....)

Pirates: That old rogue is not going to treat us like this. (Pirates start fighting)

Black Jim: Give me the treasure chest, you rogue. Black Jim is in charge of this island. All the treasure belongs to me. Hand it over.

Captain B: Well, I never, if it's not Old Jim. We thought you died five years ago.

Black Jim: Well, you were wrong weren't you? Hand it over ……………… ………………………………………………………………………………..

Captain B: Over my ……………………………………………………………………… You'll have none of this fine ……………………………………………… ………………………………………………………………………………...

Black Jim: ………………………………………………………………………………

(There is a wild scene of chaos and fighting. The Captain pulls a sword out and charges towards Black Jim)

Captain B: ………………………………………………………………………………

Black Jim: Take that! Biff!

Captain B: ...and that - wallop! ………………………………………………………

(Suddenly, Black Jim gives a signal and a creepy crocodile appears. He unties the prisoners and they join Black Jim's side.)

Croc: Snap!!

Captain B: Help me! There's ………………………………………………………… ………………………………………………………………………………

Croc: ………………………………………………………………………………

Captain B: ……………………………………………………………………………… ……………………………………………………………………………… ………………………………………………………………………………

Black Jim: ……………………………………………………………………………… ………………………………………………………………………………

(There's a chase… a mischievous monkey and a hideous spider – a fearsome lobster – a terrifying crab also join in. They grab Captain Bloodthirsty and his men and …)

(Polly and Pete see their chance. They run towards the boat.)

Pete: It's difficult to walk. I'm sinking down.

Polly: We shouldn't have crossed this bog ………………..................
……………...

Pete: Well, it's better than going through the pit of poisonous snakes in the Forest Of Fear.

Pete: The main thing is that we get away from those savage pirates.

Polly: Wait! I need to fly back.

Pete: But, what on earth do you need to get?

(Polly flies off squawking and brings some treasure back in her beak. They run to the boat, climb aboard and lower the Jolly Roger. All the prisoners follow them.)

Pete: Come quickly. We need to get away at high tide.

Prisoners: ………………………………………………………………………...
………………………………………………………………………...

(They get into the boat and sail away leaving Captain Bloodthirsty and Black Jim waving furiously on the beach. They sail to England where Pete marries his sweetheart. The play ends with a wedding.)

Think of some other endings:

- An ominous monkey kidnaps the pirates and steals the treasure - but eventually Pete and Polly escape.

Can you think of any more endings?

Save our Tree

"This is Anya from G.P.E. News at nine o'clock. The residents of a small picturesque village, called Oakville, are fuming tonight because the local government is planning to remove an old tree, which has been a landmark in the village for more than 200 years.

They have barricaded the road with heavy logs. Now they are having a candlelight vigil around the tree, to prevent officials from entering the village after dark to remove it. Lets go now to our broadcaster, Kirsten, who is broadcasting live in the center of the village."

"Good Evening, Anya. Well, I have here with me the leader of the committee, who is leading the protest. Why are you so outraged about the removal of an old tree?"

"Well, the city council did not tell us that they planned to cut down the tree until two days ago. Everybody loves that tree, which has been a landmark in our village for 200 years. It is a beautiful tree. People sit in the shade of its leafy branches in the summer and eat lunch.

More than this, though, it has historical associations. Some say it was planted to mark a site where an important battle took place so it means a lot to us."

"You have a good turn out of supporters. Many people must feel very strongly about this issue. Will you stay here all night?"

"Certainly, we plan to form a human circle around the tree until the city council changes its mind. We will not give in."

We'll just hear the views of a few protesters ...

"I have climbed to the top and there is an incredible view. I'm prepared to stay all night to fight this."

"The tree is home to so many birds and animals. It just cannot be right to take away their homes."

"I just can't believe the government is even thinking of cutting down a two hundred year old tree! It just cannot be allowed."

"It has special memories for us older people. We have had parties and celebrated events under it. Although, I'm not old enough to remember when it was planted!"

"Oakville won't have the same character if there's no tree. That's why I'm prepared to fight this all the way."

"I just love this tree because it has such pretty blossoms in the spring and in the autumn it has colorful golden leaves. It just means so much to me and to the whole village."

What do you think about the tree being chopped down? Write your view in the speech bubble...

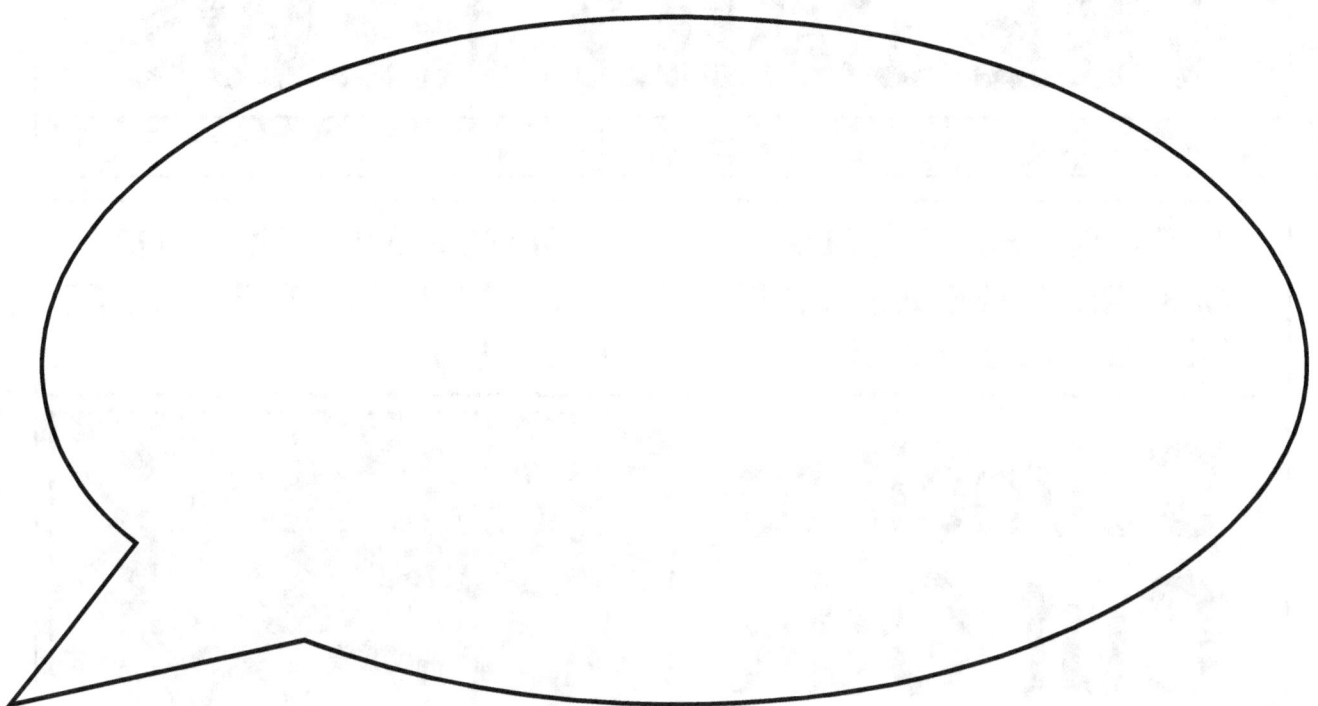

Read the newspaper article on the next page and then use the template to write your own newspaper report.

Remember:

- A headline gives you a quick summary of what the article is about. It catches the reader's attention and makes him or her want to read on. The subheading expands on the headline. It is in bold font.
- The first paragraphs give more details about the story. They have only one or two sentences.
- The later paragraphs often include interviews or quotes from witnesses or people involved in the story.
  The last paragraph summarizes the article and usually includes the writer's own comments and opinions.
- Newspaper articles are written in third person. A range of different tenses are used (present, past, future). A variety of sentence types are used. Headlines use emotive words to draw the reader in. Newspaper articles use facts, opinions, direct speech and reported speech.

EXCLUSIVE NEWS TODAY   January 22nd 2020

THE DAILY NEWS

ALL ABOUT THE BIG WORLD WE LIVE IN

TWO HUNDRED YEAR OLD OAK TREE TO BE DESTROYED. VILLAGE IN OUTRAGE!

LEADING ENVIRONMENTALIST TELLS US ABOUT THE WILDLIFE IN DANGER.

Council to Cut Oak

Residents in Dispute with City Council

By Anya Smith

The beautiful picturesque village of Oakville is still under siege tonight, as angry residents protest about the removal of their 200 year old tree.

The oak tree, which marks a historical site where a battle took place, was to be removed today.

The angry villagers have not only barricaded all the local roads with logs, but are standing around the tree refusing to move.

The council were chopping down the tree to make way for some new car parking spaces, to ease traffic congestion in the town. Mr. Carter, representing Oakville City Council, said, "I can't believe the people of this town would prefer to have an untidy tree, with falling leaves, rather than neat new car parking spaces. It is preposterous. I don't know what all the fuss is about."

Miss Patel said, "If they chop down our beautiful tree, our village will not be the same. It will look like a concrete jungle, like all the other modern towns.
If anyone feels strongly about keeping the tree, please sign the petition, which is available in the library and many local shops."

Picture: Oakville Tree

EXCLUSIVE NEWS TODAY   January 22nd 2020

THE DAILY NEWS
ALL ABOUT THE BIG WORLD WE LIVE IN

..............(Headline)..............
....
....

....
....
....

Council to ....

Residents in ....
....

By ....

The people who live in the .... village of .... are angry because the council intend to..

(Include main details - where, what, why, which, when.)

(Write in short paragraphs of 1 or 2 sentences.)

(Add further background information.)

(Include quotes)

(Use a photo to add interest. Write a caption to explain the photo.)

Picture: Oakville Tree

Mrs. Jones commented, "......................
....
....
....
....

Anna and Nick explained, "....................
....

(Include a writer's comment.)

Mrs. Barker, a teacher in the local school, is also angry about the chopping down of one of her local trees. She gets her class to write some letters to the city council and she puts the best ones up on the wall.

The children have been learning how to write an argument with 2 sides. They put forward:

a) their **own point of view**

b) **the opposite point of view**, as they argue against the council's view.

Read the following letters. Underline the arguments against chopping down the tree in red and the opposite viewpoint in blue.

Your address,
town,
state.
date

City Council Offices

Dear Sir or Madam,

I am writing to complain about the council's proposal to cut down the tree on Oakville Village Green. The council thinks it would be good for this town to chop down our special tree and to replace it with a few car parking spaces. Do we not already have a parking lot that is empty?

Everyone in our village loves the tree. It has been there for over two hundred years, since it was planted on the historical site where an important battle took place. It is photographed in guide books and people come from all over the world to see it.

More than this, it has special memories for everyone, especially elderly people who live in the town. On special occasions, like the Fourth of July, the whole village has parties under the tree. Where will we go if there is no tree?

Yours faithfully,
Aidan

Your address,
....
....

City Council Offices

Dear Sir or Madam,

I am writing to complain about the council's plans to cut down the tree on Oakville Village Green. The council thinks our tree is old and it looks untidy, especially in the autumn, when all the leaves come tumbling down. This is not right, because everyone in the village thinks that the tree is beautiful. Photographers come to take pictures of it and artists sit and paint it.

They also think that we would rather have more car parking spaces than our tree. They are completely wrong. The people in our town do not want any cars in the center; they want a safe pedestrian zone. There is already a parking lot on the edge of the village.

City officials also state that the tree is too shady and that it blocks out sunlight from the pavement. However, people do not want to sit in the hot sun. They like to sit in the shade under the leafy branches and eat picnics. Young children play tag around the tree and some of the older ones even climb it to see the view. Does that not prove that we love our tree?

Yours faithfully,
Sienna

Your address,
....
....

City Council Offices

Dear Sir or Madam,

I am writing to complain about the council's plans to chop down the tree on Oakville Village Green. Our tree is a very special tree because it is home to wildlife. There are thousands of insects - that we can't even see - living in the branches of the tree. If we chop the tree down, they will lose their homes.

There are also many birds that make their nests in our tree. Some of them migrate here, from far away, to build their nests and rear babies. You say the tree is old and untidy but it is a beautiful place, where all these creatures spend their summer. I love to watch the squirrels playing there.

You say you would prefer to see new parking lots with a parking meter installed. That will make all the people who live here very disappointed, because they won't be able to watch the squirrels darting about in the branches, the birds taking worms to their nests and big stag beetles hiding in the leaves. What would we rather have - our tree or the new parking spaces? I think you know!

Yours faithfully,
Paige

Now write your own letter to the city council, complaining about plans to cut down Oakville's tree.

Present your point of view.

State your views strongly and develop your argument.

You can:

- Present an opposite point of view and then argue against it.

- Present the opposite point of view, argue against it, present another, argue against it and so on.

- Refer to the opposite point of view as you present your point of view.

Use:

- **Rhetorical questions**
  Use a rhetorical question that doesn't need an answer but makes the reader think - Don't we already have an empty parking lot?

- Use **linking words** to link ideas (like 'more than this')

- Make the opening sentence interesting. Refer to it when writing your conclusion.

- A **topic sentence** is the name of the first sentence in the paragraph. It tells what the paragraph will be about. Other sentences in the paragraph explain the topic sentence.

Cut up the prompts on the next pages. Use them to help you structure your letter to the council. Choose which viewpoints you want to use in your letter. Lay them out on a table. Choose at least 3 points supporting the council's view and 3 points supporting the opposite viewpoint.

Beginning Paragraph: I am writing to complain about the council's decision to chop down the oak tree on Oakville Village Green. The tree is due to be cut on ... by ... and the villagers were not told about this until ... Everyone is furious.

The council proposes to chop down the tree and replace it with ...

The council considers the tree to be old and unsafe.

Officials think the tree is too shady and blocks out light in the ...

When leaves fall from the tree in autumn, the sidewalks get messy/slippery.

It is more useful to have car parking spaces than a tree.

The tree looks untidy and spoils the view by the ...

Many insect species will lose their habitat if the tree is chopped down.

Our tree is home to many species of wildlife.

The publisher permits you to copy the pages containing cut out story prompts. No other pages of this book may be copied.

- Birds rear their chicks and nest in the tree.

- People will miss the squirrels that dart up and down the tree trunk and...

- Everyone loves the tree.

- It is a landmark in the village.

- The tree is planted on a historic site where...

- The people who live in the village do not want cars in the center because...

- There is already a huge parking lot on the edge of the village which is...

- Villagers want the center to be a safe pedestrian zone.

- The tree looks colorful in the autumn.

- Young children like to play tag around the tree or climb...

Elderly people remember having parties around the tree when...

Oakville will have to be called a different name because...

People come to see it from all over the country.

Artists sit and paint the tree.

People have picnics under the tree.

Photographers take pictures of the tree, because they think it is beautiful.

It has been in our village for...

Final Paragraph: Finally, the people of Oakville intend to stop the contractor from cutting the tree down by...They have signed a petition to say...

Yours faithfully,

....

The publisher permits you to copy the pages containing cut out story prompts. No other pages of this book may be copied.

....
....
....
....

Dear Sir or Madam,

I am writing to complain that the council is planning to cut down our ....
....
....
....
....
....
....
....
....
....
....
....
....
....
....

Yours faithfully,

....

Ollie tries writing a 'rap' about the old oak tree being cut down. What do you think of his effort? Does it have rhyming couplets? Why not try writing a rap or a poem of your own or improving on this one.

Let's stop the men
who sit with a pen
and make up a plan
to send in a man,
who'll cut down our tree
that everyone can see.

Where will we sit
and the old lady knit?
Where will we eat,
In the shade, on a seat,
Without the old oak tree
that everyone can see?

What about the kids
that climbed and hid?
Where will they play,
as they while away the day
with no old tree
for everyone to see?

What about the wildlife?
It causes them a lot of strife.
They'll have to find a new home.
They'll have to roam and roam
because there will be no tree to see.

What makes the council think like that?
Why don't they care about the squirrel and the bat?
They only want concrete car parking spaces,
wide pavements and shops full of laces.
They only think of money
not bees that make honey.

So let's protest and let go, go, go...
with leaflets and banners that say no, no, no...
and we'll all stand on the council land
and we'll stop the men
who sit with the pen
and make up a plan.

Can you spot the rhyming couplets?

e.g. man and plan

Think of something that you would feel strongly about if it happened in your town. Write a leaflet to explain the situation. What would you (do) (say)?

Produce the writing to go in a leaflet which will:

- <u>Point</u> out that a forest is going to be cut down to make way for a new road.
- Give some <u>evidence</u> to say why it should not happen.
- Make some <u>comments</u> that will persuade them to sign the petition.

Think about how people feel:
- Why do the council want to do this?
- Why are people angry?

People love the forest because:

- It is very old. It has historical associations.
- It is a beautiful place to go.
- People picnic under the trees.
- Children play there.
- It is home to wildlife.
- It looks colorful in autumn.

What action did people take to stop men from cutting down the forest?

Is there a petition for people to sign?

 Now produce the writing to stop...
1. A swimming pool from being closed.
2. A library or community hall from being shut down.
3. A house from being knocked down.

I love to:

- swim in the pool, to feel the salty water on my skin and ride over the powerful waves.
  (touch)

- watch a fireworks display and see the sky filled with glittering stars.
  (sight)

- eat delicious ice cream because it is so cool and creamy on my tongue.
  (taste)

- smell bonfires on a November night.
  (smell)

- hear the soft purr of my cat.
  (hearing)

- smell cheese and tomato on toast grilling.
  (smell)

- taste sizzling hot dogs with ketchup and onions.
  (taste)

- stroke my cat and feel her velvet grey fur slipping through my fingers. It is so relaxing.
  (touch)

Use **SENSES** for writing description:

**SIGHT
TOUCH
SMELL
HEARING
TASTE**

To impact your reader.

- fly through the air on a roller coaster and hear the people screaming.
  (hearing)

- go on scary rides, to be hurtled through the air fast and be turned upside down.
  (feel)

- look down from a plane and to see the fields like squares below.
  (sight)

- have my arm grabbed by a spooky creature on the ghost train. It sends shivers up my spine.
  (touch)

- taste spicy food that is hot, hot, hot like curry - yum, yum!
  (taste)

- smell the scent of freshly cut grass in the summer.
  (smell)

- smell the floral scent of my bath oil filling the air with perfume.
  (smell)

What do you like?
Why?
Add your own ideas.

But, **I hate**:

- to hear the same C.D. played over and over again on boring car trips.
  (hearing)

- stingy wasps that buzz around your food when you eat outside.
  (hearing)

- stringy, green beans that get stuck in your teeth and disgusting Brussels sprouts that taste awful.
  (taste)

- to have soggy, wet socks after I have stepped in a puddle.
  (touch)

- minty toothpaste, especially when it slips and slides off the brush and down the drain.
  (taste)

- creepy, old houses that are haunted by ghoulish ghosts and fearsome phantoms, that make shivers go up my spine.
  (touch)

- deafening bangs of thunder and brilliant strokes of lightning, that light up your bedroom as you curl up in bed trying to sleep.
  (hear)

Sam says,

"I hate being told off by my teacher when I haven't done my homework."

"You are a lazy, foolish and naughty boy," she shouts.

"I hate it when the internet shuts down on my computer. I have to wait and wait for it to start up again."

"I hate being moaned at by the lunch lady for talking in the line."

"Mom hates the smell of the bottom of my school bag, when it is full of squishy bananas, rotting apples and half eaten bags of chips."

"Most of all, I hate the sound of rain that drip, drip, drips down your neck into your sweatshirt and makes you shudder."

What do you hate?
Why?
Add your own ideas.

Danny writes an argument on…

I hate long trips in the car.

I hate boring trips in our minivan. When my parents drive to Florida or California it takes hours and hours – in fact it can take more than 20 hours. It is a 'long haul' drive. If I'd gone by plane, I'd be in Australia!

Here are some of the reasons I hate being squashed up in the back of the minivan with all the luggage:

- My dad listens to the same old C.D. over and over again. If you want a clue how old it is – the rock band split up over fifteen years ago.

- The second reason is that Dad always takes the same route along the boring highway; looking out onto the same flat, green fields I saw last year. I ask myself, why can't we take the exciting mountain route we drove the first time we came? Incidentally, we got lost and drove over some amazing mountain passes, with huge drops into the valley below. Amazing views! Hard to say, but I think Dad got scared.

- Thirdly, I do not like the voice on my Dad's GPS – so dull. I wonder why we can't have a funky voice of a pop star singing out directions – that would be more fun. That GPS lady pretends to be an authority on getting to a place, but she doesn't even know where construction is happening or where the detour is or where roads are closed. What does she know?

- Finally, I don't like any of the travel toys my mom buys me. I read the magazines in the first half an hour, the little chess pieces from my compact travel game fall over the floor and I'm bored of the crossword puzzles after ten minutes. What's more, I nearly always pack my iPod away in my suitcase, which is on the roof rack, and the batteries are always dead on my DVD player and Mom never remembers to bring some spare ones. Do parents ever think of us kids?

That is why I do not like long trips.

Flying is Fabulous

I think flying is fabulous. First, it is just fun checking in at the airport, showing my passport at customs and putting my luggage on the conveyor belt to go through the security check. It is funny when Dad is patted down, because the alarm has gone off. The duty free shops are fun to wander around, while you keep an eye on the boarding screen. Then I get a thrill when a voice calls over the speaker, 'Flight… is now boarding. Please have your boarding passes ready.' The crew greets us as we board the plane and we find our seats and space for our luggage.

Next, I like take-off. The best part is when the plane taxis down the runway. It goes slowly at first, but then the pilot increases speed and we go hurtling down the runway and lift off into the air like a bird. The plane rises like an eagle, soaring high; the buildings below get smaller and smaller, like a Lego toy town below. Amazing! Then, we climb up to the airways. The sky is blue and I can see fluffy clouds beneath me like little bits of cotton wool. The seat belt sign goes off and the crew starts to bustle around.

After this, I like to watch a film and then read a bit of Dad's newspaper. As I search up and down the aisle to check on the progress of dinner, I take a sip of my lemonade but… it has spilled all over another passenger. It is not my fault that we are going through a storm and there is a lot of turbulence. I am almost sad when five hours have gone by and we are descending through the clouds. We are circling around and around to land, but we can't see anything because it is pouring with rain. Then, the plane's wheels touch down on the runway with just a little jolt, as the pilot lands the plane skillfully on the runway. Off we go on to the airport bus and join the lines to buy our visa. We search the luggage carousel for our baggage and clamber into a taxi to start our holiday. It's great!

 Write a story about journeys by car, plane or train.

I hate scary headlines...

Rats as BIG as Dogs Seen in the Park!

Ghostly, Headless, PHANTOM appears at FAMOUS HOUSE.

Ship Hijacked by Pirates.

Animals being stolen by thieves.

✏️ Can you think up some more scary headlines? Why don't you try and write up some of these newspaper reports. Use your imagination.

....

....

....

Kim says, "I love my favorite pop star Chelsea B," as she listens to her interview on the internet.

Where did you grow up?

I was born in the U.S.A. and I grew up in Los Angeles, where I lived in Beverly Hills and knew lots of film stars as a small child.

How old were you when you started?

I started singing when I was only eight years old and had made a number one album by the time I was twelve.

That's an amazing achievement, but you went on to record more best selling albums - didn't you?

As I grew older, I had twelve best selling albums and number one hits across the world. You know, I am a trained dancer as well as singer. I can do amazing dance routines that my fans like to copy. In recent years, I have toured the world singing my hit songs.

You have appeared in several Hollywood blockbuster movies - haven't you?

Yes, I was in three movies with another one planned for next year.

How are you feeling about yourself?

I rock! At the moment, I have long purple hair with blonde highlights, which touches my butt, but I like to re-invent my look often.

What clothes do you like to wear?

I always wear the latest and most trendy designer fashions. I'm never afraid to stand out in a crowd.

There you go. Thanks to Chelsea B. She is so cool!

 Imagine you meet your favorite pop star. Now make up some questions that you would like to ask him/her. Write the replies you think they would give.

Now it's your turn to write.

- Who is your favorite pop star?
- Where was he/she born?
- What do you know about his or her childhood?
- What hits has he/she had?
- What albums has he/she recorded?
- Has he/she done a world tour?
- Have you seen him/her on tour/in concert?
- When did you see the concert?
- Where did you see it?
- Did you enjoy the concert?

- Who are your favorite celebrities?
- Are they film stars, T.V. stars, soap stars, actors or actresses?
- What do you know about them?
- Write down details about where they were born.
- What did they do as a child or as a young adult?
- How did they become famous?
- What are they doing now?
- If you could meet them, what would you ask them?

You can use the internet or a magazine or book to help you research your favorite celebrity.

Now it's your turn to write about your favorite T.V. show.

> Sam says, "I tune into The Fab Days of Mack and Jody every night on T.V. after dinner. The stars are my age. It is about their life living in a space ship. They have daring adventures like the time they found a robot in the closet. They were really scared because it escaped and it was going to take over the world. Then they managed to capture it with the help of all their friends."

- What channel is it on?

- Who appears in it?

- What do you know about them?

- What is the program about?

Write about your favorite episode.

- How did it begin?

- What happened next?

- How did it end?

Read the story on the next page.

Write a story about something you have done with a friend. Use dialogue to move the story on.

We love winning, but we hate to lose.

Every year the kids at Melissa Montague's School of Dance enter the choreography competition. They make up dances to perform on stage; the best one wins a medal and the chance to perform their number in the annual show.

"Let's look through the old CD's and choose a piece of music," said Yasmin excitedly.
"A nice catchy number with a good beat. What about this?"
"Definitely not!"
"...or this one?"
"No! We did that last year."
"...But, that would be amazing. Let's try it."

We spent all morning making up a dance.
"Come here Mom," I yelled. "Watch this."
"I'm busy," she yelled.
"It won't take a minute."
"OK," she said, popping her head around the door. She watched for a minute.
"Wow, that's really good, you could be on 'America's Got Talent'..."

The day of the competition arrived. We stood at the side of the stage waiting to go on. It was scary.
"Your turn," beckoned Annie, the dancing teacher. "Go up on stage." We took up our positions ready to dance, but nothing happened. We waited: still no music.
"There's a bit of a technical problem, I think," exclaimed Annie. She fiddled with the switches of the CD player. The music filled the room and we started our dance... but the CD player started to splutter... and the music stopped...
"I don't know what's wrong with this machine today," added Annie impatiently.

Two hours later we waited nervously for the results.
"We were on stage for ten minutes," whispered Yasmin to Lara.
"It was so scary. By the time they got the music going, I got so nervous I did it all wrong."
"Me too."
"Do we stand any chance?"
"Not much. Those new girls were amazing." We waited with baited breath. Miss Annie stood up and a hush went around the room.
"The standard was so high this year we couldn't choose, so we decided to award everyone a medal. Since we only have a few contestants, you can all do your numbers in the show. Well done," she added. "You are all winners..."

Guinea Pig Education can help you use **punctuation** in *your* writing.

Let's get going!

First, don't forget to **write in sentences**. Use **capital letters** and **periods**.

Jules belongs to **S**ydney at 12 **O**live **G**rove, **R**ushford.

Now try this one:

lois and lulu belong to anya at 14 chesterfield gardens rushford

---

Use a **!**

That's exciting!
What a surprise!
Oh bother!

Use a **?**

What do guinea pigs eat?

Hold out a piece of vegetable. Will your guinea pig eat it?

Now try this one:

guinea pigs like to be stroked do they bite they are timid but rarely bite ouch

---

Do not forget to use "**.....**" when you use **direct speech**.

"Anya, what did you buy at the pet shop?" said Jules.
"I bought a cage, some straw, some hay, a bowl, a water bottle and some food for my new guinea pigs."

Use commas for **Lists**.

Use commas **before or after** a **phrase** or subordinate **clause** in a sentence.

Use commas **around a clause hidden** in the **middle of a complex sentence**.

Try these:

Lois is lively inquisitive and nosy

Guinea pigs can be chocolate black silver white and tortoise shell.

My guinea pig called Jules has long hair.

After cleaning the cage Anya put in some hay.

Try these: *(answers on next page)*

What is your guinea pig like anya

Lulu has a white coat, uneven colored spots and black ears she replied

After running in the grass Jules dozed in his hutch.

Guinea Pigs in the wild live in a burrow.

Some guinea pigs with long hair have rosettes.

Let's remember **apostrophes**:

> The carrot belonging to Jules is **Jules's carrot.**

> The hutch of Lois and Lulu is the **guinea pigs' hutch.**

Plus, remember apostrophes for shortened words.

> They are gorgeous.
> **They're** gorgeous.

Try these:

> The guinea pig belongs to Kate.
>
> The hutch of the rabbits George and Ginger.
>
> Isnt he sweet.

Finally, you can use a **colon** in a list.

> Jess had five smart guinea pigs: a short haired coat, a long coarse coat, a deep shining coat, a smooth coat and one with rosettes and twirls.

Or you can use a **semicolon** to separate two similar ideas in a list.

> Guinea pigs are sociable; they like company.

Try this:
> The male guinea pig is a boar the female is a sow.

Make a sentence with a :
Make a sentence with a ;

For extra information you may need to use a **dash** for a longer pause.

> Dad bought Anya a guinea pig - it was so sweet.
>
> Jules nibbled his carrot loudly - crunch, crunch, crunch.

Or you could use **parentheses** for extra information.

> The guinea pigs (Lois and Lulu) scampered across the grass.

Try these:

> Anya fed her guinea pig he was hungry.
>
> The rabbits George and Ginger are great friends.

How did you do?

- Lois and Lulu belong to Anya at 14 Chesterfield Gardens, Rushford.
- Guinea pigs like to be stroked. Do they bite? They are timid but rarely bite. Ouch!
- Lois is lively, inquisitive and nosy.
- Guinea pigs can be chocolate, black, silver, white and tortoise shell.
- My guinea pig, called Jules, has long hair.
- After cleaning the cage, Anya put in some hay.
- "What is your guinea pig like Anya?"
  "Lulu has a white coat, uneven colored spots and black ears," she replied.
- After running in the grass, Jules dozed in his hutch.
- Guinea pigs, in the wild, live in a burrow.
- Some guinea pigs, with long hair, have rosettes.
- Kate's guinea pig/ the rabbits' hutch/ Isn't he sweet.
- Anya fed her guinea pig - he was hungry.
- The rabbits (George and Ginger) are great friends.
- The male guinea pig is a boar; the female is a sow.

Aren't I sweet?

Of course!

Guinea Pig **Spelling** *Tips*

Guinea pig says, "Don't forget it is important to read through your writing, so you can spot any obvious mistakes. Here are a few basic spelling tips. Make sure you can spell all the words on these pages."

Tricky homophones

Homophones sound the same but are spelled differently.

*I gave **two** carrots **to** Jules but he's getting **too** fat.*

***Our** guinea pigs **are** cute.*

*They're over **there** by **their** hutch.*

Difficult Endings

Some words have tricky endings.

*The **latch** on Jules's **hutch** comes open. He gets out and eats a **patch** of grass by the **hedge**. I try to **catch** him but he **dodges** me and runs off.*

*When I **handle** my little piggy, I **cuddle** him.*

Some words have spelling rules.

You double the final letter of a verb with a short sound.

*I **hug** Jules.*
*I am **hugging** him.*

*I **pat** the rabbit.*
*I am **patting** him.*

*I **grab** him.*
*I am **grabbing** hold of him.*

*He **hops**.*
*He is **hopping**.*

If the final letter is a consonant, just add the ending.

*He **licks**.*
*He is **licking**.*

*He **fights**.*
*He is **fighting**.*

*I **hold** him.*
*I am **holding** him.*

Drop the 'e' if you are adding an ending with a vowel.

*I **love** my guinea pig.*
*I am **loving** him.*

*I **stroke** my guinea pig.*
*I am **stroking** him.*

*He is having an **adventure**.*
*He is **adventurous**.*

Use the same rule for:

shine   shiny
noise   noisy

But, if the ending begins with a consonant you keep the 'e':

live	lively
love	lovely
lone	lonely
safe	safely

When you add an ending some words change the 'y' to an 'i':

*My guinea pig is **happy**.*
*He is **happier**.*
*He is the **happiest**.*

busy	busier	busiest
cry	cries	cried
piggy	piggies	
carry	carries	carried

	Comparative	Superlative
He is fast.	faster	the fastest
He is fine.	finer	the finest
He is a beauty.	more beautiful	most beautiful

Use Sounds

ch, sh, wh, th, oo, ee, ar, or, ur, ir, er, e, ai, ay, oi, oy, oa, ow, ou, au, aw, ce, ci, cy, ge, gi, gy, short y, long y, magic e...

... to sound out 80% of words.

Use syllables to sound out hard words.

Eat **VEG ET ABLES**
Soft 'g' - ge, gi, gy.

are **COM FORT ABLE**

like **MIX TURE**

have an **AD VEN TURE**

SEV EN

PRECIOUS

CREATURE

Remember:

1. Sound hard words out using syllables.

2. Jot down words you find difficult. Learn them.

3. Use a dictionary or thesaurus.

Don't forget to keep your writing neat. Small letters should be the same height. There should be one little finger space between each word.

Make sure you can write this passage:

My guinea pigs feed on green leaves. They munch, crunch, scratch, scrunch in their hutch. Early in the morning it is necessary to feed them healthy food and fill up the water container. My noisy young pigs enjoy playing excitedly in their run on the lawn, where they are safe from danger.

Really tricky ones:

'i' before 'e' except after 'c' - when the sound is ee.

believe

fierce

field

conceited

Exceptions:

neighbor

Silent Letters:

Guinea Pigs:

gnaw

clim**b**

eat crum**b**s

are caut**i**ous

are ca**l**m

are **k**nowing

wrinkle up their noses

Tricky words:

Are you **tough enough** to keep a guinea pig?

They can't be **caught**.

They fill one with **laughter**.

They love to be **photographed**.

Guinea pig says, "Make lists of tricky words you find difficult from the groups of words."

The glossary

A starting point:	is something that gives you an idea to write a story.
The genre is:	the type of story you choose to write. It could be a traditional tale, that has a message that good overcomes evil, or a romance, horror, fantasy, mystery, realistic or adventure story.
Planning a story:	Structuring the story into three or more paragraphs – with a beginning, a middle and an ending.
Characters:	are people who feature in the story – we learn how they behave and about their feelings, motives, emotions and conflicts.
A setting:	is the place where the story takes place - creating a mood.
The plot:	is a sequence of events that make up the story. Action in the story may be triggered by a conflict, complication, problem, or unexpected event that needs to be solved.
Suspense:	is built up to leave the reader guessing what will happen. Use: • short sentences for impact – 'Help!' • show the feelings of the characters – 'suddenly his heart missed a beat' – to build up a dramatic climax that leaves the reader on the edge of his chair wondering how it will end.
First person:	tells the story, using 'I' or 'we' – so the reader can imagine being the main character.
Second person:	uses 'you' and speaks directly to the reader or involves the reader.
Third person:	uses 'he,' 'she,' 'it,' 'they' to tell the story as a narrator, like a fly on the wall watching.
Atmosphere:	is the mood and feeling conjured up in the story.
Flashback:	if you start your story with action, you may include a few details about what went on before.
Ending or resolution:	may be happy, sad, moral (a lesson learned) or a cliffhanger - where the reader imagines his or her own ending.

Paragraphs:	start a new line (one finger space in for handwriting). Use a new paragraph if you change event, time or place.
Conjunctions:	are linking words that start paragraphs or join sentences. Examples are: as, since, because, but, if, then, so, as a result of, for instance, yet, after a while, suddenly.
Dialogue:	is what people say and can move the story on. Use correct punctuation – *Lilly said, "Is it hot in here?"* (direct speech); *Lilly said that it was hot in here.* (indirect or reported speech)
The opening:	is the first sentence of a story - fiction or narrative.
A topic sentence:	is the first sentence in a paragraph, which tells the reader what it will be about. Further sentences will develop the idea and explain it.
Describe:	is making a word picture.
Adjective and noun:	*shimmering sand* (describing word, naming word)
Verb and adverb:	*shouting noisily* (action word, describes action word)
Powerful verbs and adverbs:	Choosing key words - *'a voice sounded mysteriously,' 'he nodded his head anxiously.'*
Similes:	compare using as and like – *'as white as snow'*
Metaphors:	compare two similar things, but don't use like or as. *'The dog was a little monster.'*
Script:	tells a story through the characters' dialogue.

Writers' techniques	include:
	   * repetition
	   * rhetorical questions - questions that don't need an answer
	   * personification - giving an object human qualities
	   * onomatopoeia - words that sound like their name
	   * alliteration - several words that start with the same letter

Fiction:	includes story and narrative.
Non-fiction:	includes information, diaries, leaflets, reports, recounts, descriptions.
Purpose:	why it is written – to inform, explain, describe, persuade, advise or argue.
Target audience:	are the people the article is written for – to instruct someone on how to use a ..., to explain how to get somewhere, to persuade or convince the reader to do something.

www.ingramcontent.com/pod-product-compliance
Lightning Source LLC
Chambersburg PA
CBHW050714090526
44587CB00019B/3380